HOUSTON
ASTROS

by J Chris Roselius

Published by ABDO Publishing Company, 8000 West 78th Street, Edina, Minnesota 55439.

Printed in the United States of America,
North Mankato, Minnesota
112010
012011

THIS BOOK CONTAINS AT LEAST 10% RECYCLED MATERIALS.

Editor: Matt Tustison
Copy Editor: Nicholas Cafarelli
Interior Design and Production: Carol Castro
Cover Design: Kazuko Collins

Photo Credits: Morry Gash/AP Images, cover; Pat Sullivan/AP Images, title, 8, 47; James A. Finley/AP Images, 4, 43 (bottom); David J. Phillip/AP Images, 7, 33, 34; Darron Cummings/AP Images, 10; Houston Chronicle/AP Images, 12; Photo by Focus on Sport/Getty Images, 15, 24, 42 (top); JPK/AP Images, 16; Houston Astros/AP Images, 18; Charles E. Knoblock/AP Images, 21; DY/AP Images, 22; Photo by Ronald C. Modra/Sports Imagery/Getty Images, 27, 42 (middle); Susan Ragan/AP Images, 29, 42 (bottom); Getty Images, 30; Brett Coomer/AP Images, 36, 43 (top); John Bazemore/AP Images, 39, 43 (middle); Wilfredo Lee/AP Images, 41; Tim Johnson/AP Images, 44

Library of Congress Cataloging-in-Publication Data
Roselius, J Chris
Houston Astros / by J Chris Roselius.
p. cm. — (Inside MLB)
Includes index.
ISBN 978-1-61714-045-7
1. Houston Astros (Baseball team)—History—Juvenile literature. I. Title.
GV875.H64R67 2011
796.357'64097641411—dc22
2010036565

TABLE OF CONTENTS

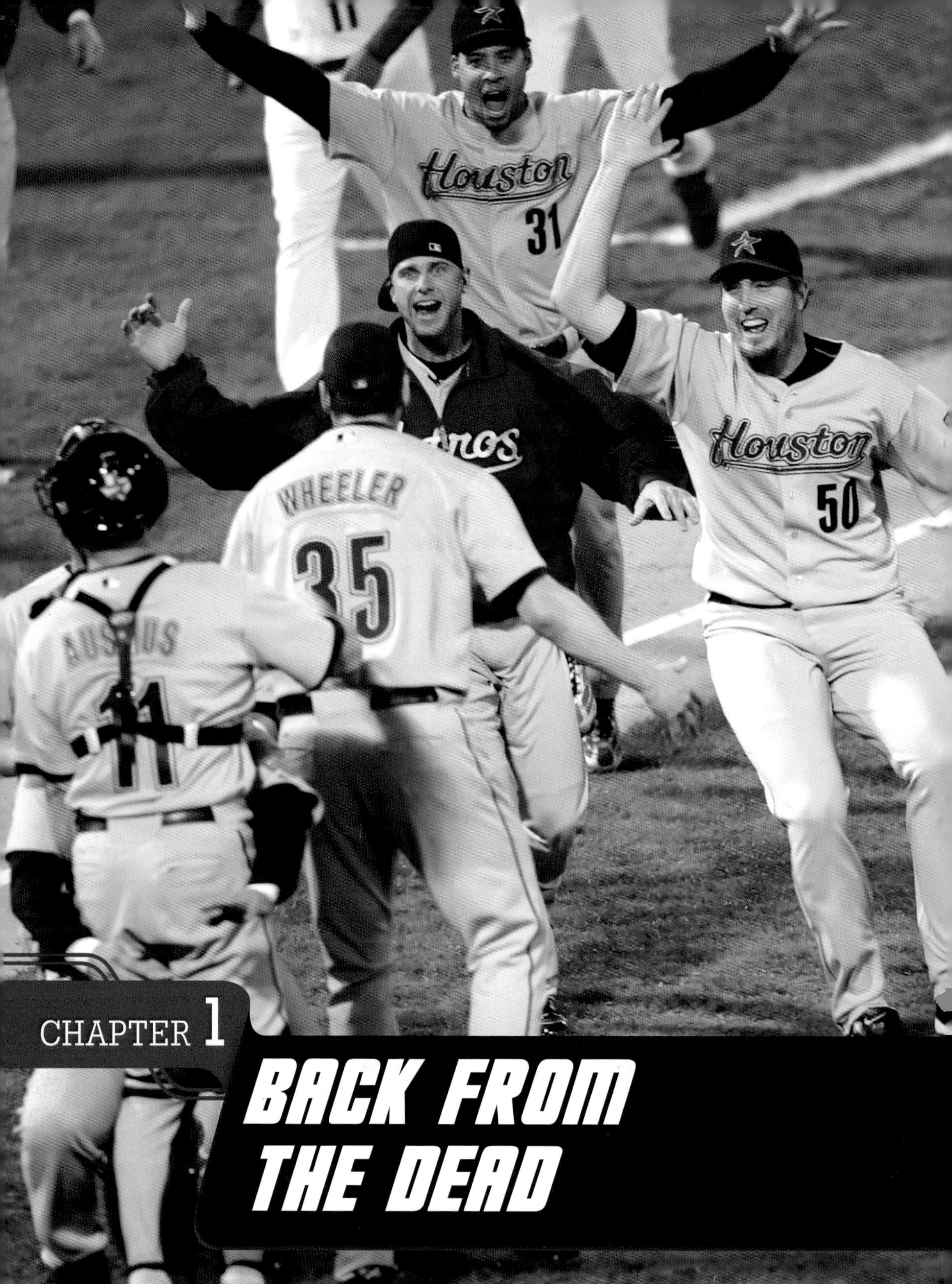

CHAPTER 1
BACK FROM THE DEAD

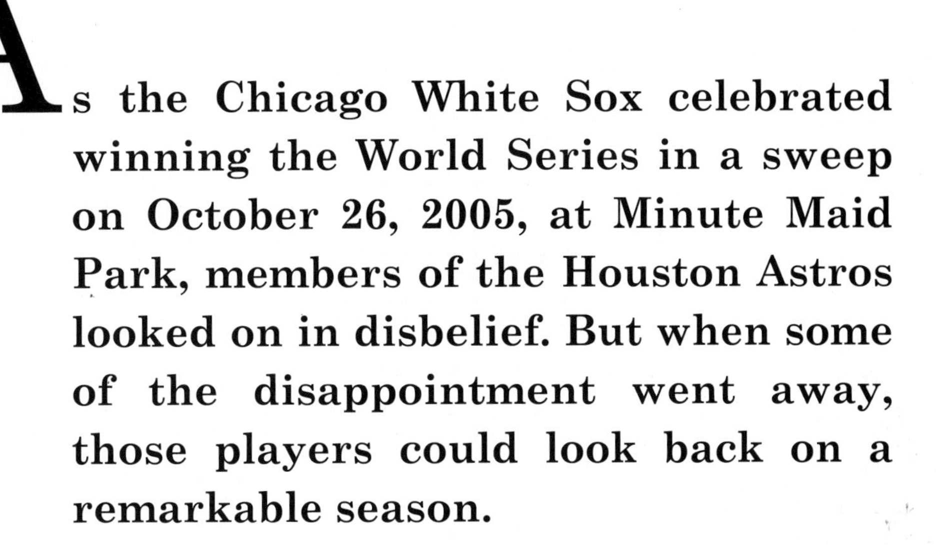

As the Chicago White Sox celebrated winning the World Series in a sweep on October 26, 2005, at Minute Maid Park, members of the Houston Astros looked on in disbelief. But when some of the disappointment went away, those players could look back on a remarkable season.

Remarkable is a good word to describe the Astros' presence in their first World Series that season. It was the National League (NL) team's 44th year in the major leagues. Entering the season, Houston had to fill gaps. They were created by key player departures and injuries. Center fielder Carlos Beltran signed with the New York Mets. He had helped lift the Astros to the NL Championship Series (NLCS) in 2004. Second baseman Jeff Kent also was not re-signed. He was the team leader in runs batted in (RBIs) in 2004. All-Star slugger

Astros players, including Brad Ausmus (11), Dan Wheeler (35), and Chad Qualls (50), celebrate after the team won the 2005 NLCS.

Lance Berkman started the year on the disabled list because of an off-season knee injury.

The Astros won four of their first five games in 2005 but then slumped. By the end of April, Houston was just 9–13. On May 5, longtime first baseman Jeff Bagwell said he would undergo surgery on his injured right shoulder. The procedure could possibly knock him out for the rest of the season. Berkman returned to the lineup. But he struggled at the plate after missing all of spring training as well as April.

On May 24, the Astros fell to 15–30. Days later, the *Houston Chronicle* newspaper ran an article in the sports section displaying a giant tombstone. The message was that it was time to bury the Astros. The 1914 Boston Braves were the last team to make the postseason after falling 15 games under .500. Some fans thought that the Astros were done. General manager Tim Purpura disagreed, though. To him, it was just a matter of time before the team got on a hot streak.

"I thought that it was extremely premature," Purpura said when he first saw the giant tombstone. " . . . I guess I was right."

As if on cue, Berkman and Morgan Ensberg picked up the

Pitching In

One reason that the Astros did not panic when they started the 2005 season 15–30 was because of their strong pitching staff. Roy Oswalt, Roger Clemens, and Andy Pettitte kept the Astros in nearly every game in which they pitched. Oswalt finished the season 20–12 with a 2.94 earned-run average (ERA). Clemens was 13–8 with an NL-leading 1.37 ERA. Pettitte went 17–9 with a 2.39 ERA. Clemens, the NL Cy Young Award winner in 2004, finished third in the voting in 2005. Oswalt was fourth, and Pettitte placed fifth.

Roger Clemens delivers a pitch in 2005. Clemens was part of a talented pitching staff that helped Houston rocket back into contention after a poor start that season.

pace at the plate. Jason Lane also found his stroke. Lane hit eight home runs and drove in 18 runs in June. Houston climbed to within six games of .500 at the end of that month. Then, the Astros really took off. In July, they won 22 of 29 games to improve to 57–48. Finally, Houston sprinted to a 19–11 finish over its last 30 games of the regular season.

In the final game of the season, the Astros defeated the visiting Chicago Cubs 6–4. Houston finished the season 89–73. The team clinched the NL's wild-card playoff berth.

Roy Oswalt pitches in the regular-season finale on October 2, 2005, against the Cubs. Oswalt earned his 20th victory of the season as the Astros won 6–4 and clinched a playoff spot.

Roy Oswalt earned the win in the last game. He reached 20 victories for the second straight season. Bagwell played a key role as a pinch-hitter in the team's go-ahead rally in the sixth inning. He had returned from the disabled list on September 9.

For the fifth time in their six NL Division Series (NLDS) appearances, the Astros would face the Atlanta Braves. Houston won the series three games to one. The Astros prevailed in an amazing Game 4. The contest lasted 18 innings. It was the longest postseason game in major league history. Chris Burke ended the game with a home run to left field in the bottom of the 18th.

The Astros advanced to the NLCS. They faced the St. Louis Cardinals for the second year in a row. Houston avenged its 2004 series loss. This was thanks in large part to two strong starts from Oswalt. The right-hander was named the Most Valuable Player (MVP) of the NLCS. Oswalt was the winner in Houston's series-clinching 5–1 road victory in Game 6. The Astros had earned a spot in the World Series for the first time.

"I'm not greedy, I'm not selfish, just wanted to go one time [to the World Series]. I can't tell you how happy I am," said veteran Houston second baseman Craig Biggio. Biggio had broken into the major leagues with the Astros in 1988.

"Exactly the Right Time"

The Astros' amazing comeback was special for Houston in 2005. But that year will also be remembered for the way the city opened its hearts and homes. Hurricane Katrina ripped through New Orleans, Louisiana, in August 2005. The next month, Hurricane Rita arrived in East Texas, not far from Houston. Katrina was the more damaging of the two storms, greatly affecting New Orleans. That city is located just a few hundred miles away from Houston. Houston welcomed approximately 150,000 evacuees from New Orleans and turned out nearly 100,000 volunteers to help them find food and shelter. "Houston—and Texas—waited a long time for the World Series, and it came to us at exactly the right time," then-Houston mayor Bill White said. "I can't describe the tremendous lift it gave us. . . . The chance it gave Houstonians . . . to pull together was like manna from baseball heaven."

Craig Biggio, who had been an Astro since 1988, hits a run-scoring single during the clinching Game 6 of the 2005 NLCS.

Unfortunately for the Astros, they ran into a very hot White Sox team in the World Series. Chicago had not won the Series since 1917. The White Sox were on a mission.

In the World Series, two games were decided by one run. The difference in both of the other games was just two runs. But the White Sox found ways to win. This included a 7–5 victory in 14 innings in Game 3 and a 1–0 win in Game 4. Chicago held Houston to a .203 batting average in the Series.

Despite being swept, the Astros could be proud. They

had surprised many baseball followers by coming back from their slow start to the season. The 2005 World Series appearance capped a nine-season stretch in which Houston made the playoffs six times.

It was the most successful period in team history. The Astros began as an expansion franchise in 1962. The team was then known as the Houston Colt .45s. It took until the 1980s for Houston to become a consistent winner. By the next decade and into the new century, the Astros had buried their losing ways. They were ready to blast off into an era of success that, unfortunately for them, also included much postseason frustration.

BAGWELL'S LAST GAMES

First baseman Jeff Bagwell broke into the major leagues with the Astros in 1991. But it was not until 2005 that he got to play in the World Series.

Even though he missed most of the season with an injury, he was added to the postseason roster. Bagwell was the designated hitter during the first two games in Chicago. He went 1-for-8 with a run scored. His pinch-hit appearance in the bottom of the seventh inning of Game 4 in Houston would be his final at-bat as an Astro, however.

Unable to play in 2006 because of his right shoulder injury, Bagwell officially retired in December of that year. He played his entire big-league career with Houston. "I feel very proud of [that fact]," Bagwell said.

CHAPTER 2

THE BEGINNING

By the late 1950s, Houston had been trying to land a big-league baseball team for several years. In 1959, Houston and several other cities that wanted to have Major League Baseball (MLB) teams announced that they would form their own league. It would be called the Continental League and would be a rival to MLB. The new league was scheduled to begin play in 1961.

NL owners feared having to compete with a new league for fans. As a result, they granted expansion teams to Houston and New York. The Continental League broke up before a game was ever played. The addition of the Houston and New York teams gave the NL a total of 10 squads—the same number as in the AL. Houston and New York would both begin play in 1962.

The new Houston team was named the Colt .45s. The Colt .45 was known as "the gun that won the West." Navy blue and

Fans at Colt Stadium watch the Houston Colt .45s during the team's first regular-season game on April 10, 1962. Three years later, the team was renamed the Astros and moved indoors to the Astrodome.

THE ASTRODOME

Playing baseball outdoors in warm and muggy Houston during the summer was not very comfortable for players or fans of the Colt .45s.

As a result, owner Roy Hofheinz dreamed of playing baseball indoors. His dream came true with the construction of the Astrodome. A giant dome covered the baseball field and the grandstands without a single column to obstruct the views of the fans. And because the ballpark had a roof, the entire stadium was air-conditioned.

However, there were some kinks that had to be worked out. The roof consisted of 4,007 skylights, making it nearly impossible to see a fly ball when the game was played during daylight hours. The skylights were painted to block out the sun. But the grass then started to die due to the lack of sunlight. Thus came the invention of Astroturf, or artificial grass. It was installed as the playing surface in 1966.

orange were selected as the team's colors. The New York team was named the Mets.

Houston's debut season in 1962 was probably most memorable for the heat and humidity and the giant mosquitoes that the team had to endure at Colt Stadium. The Colt .45s' play on the field certainly was not very memorable. Fielding a team of castoffs from other teams and young players, Houston went 64–96 in its first season.

In 1965, the Houston club changed its name. With the birth of the National Aeronautics and Space Administration (NASA) in 1958, Houston became heavily involved with the United States' space program. Beginning in 1961, the city was home to the Manned Spacecraft Center. The center was later renamed the Johnson Space Center. The owner

The Astrodome, the "Eighth Wonder of the World," is shown in the 1980s. The domed stadium was the Astros' home from 1965 to 1999.

of the Colt .45s was Roy Hofheinz. He was Houston's mayor from 1953 to 1955 and previously served as a county judge. He changed the team's name. The new name was the Astros—short for astronauts.

The team also moved into the most modern stadium known at the time—the Astrodome. It was the world's first indoor stadium. Nicknamed the "Eighth Wonder of the World," the Astrodome featured a giant roof over the stadium. This allowed the game to be played in air-conditioning. The stadium also featured a giant scoreboard extending from left field to right field.

Center fielder Jimmy Wynn is shown in 1968. Despite his small size, the "Toy Cannon" was a powerful hitter for Houston.

By this time, the Astros were young but talented. Rookie Joe Morgan, only 21 years old, was the starter at second base. Jimmy Wynn, 23, was the center fielder. Rusty Staub, 21, was in right field. Meanwhile, the pitching staff featured 18-year-old right-hander Larry Dierker. Don Nottebart, Turk Farrell, and Bob Bruce were the other starting pitchers.

In 1969, Houston finally broke through with its first nonlosing season. The Astros finished 81–81.

Despite Houston's struggles in the 1960s, there were some nice individual accomplishments. Nottebart became the team's first pitcher to throw a no-hitter when Houston beat the visiting Philadelphia Phillies 4–1 on May 17, 1963. Don Wilson joined the Astros' starting staff as a rookie in 1967. He threw two no-hitters for the team, in 1967 and 1969.

At the plate, Morgan and Staub were becoming stars. As a rookie in 1965, Morgan hit .271 with 14 home runs, 40 RBIs, and 20 stolen bases. The next season, he was named to the NL All-Star team. Staub became the first Houston player to hit .300 when he had a .333 batting average with 10 homers and 74 RBIs in 1967. He was named to the All-Star team that season and in 1968.

Wynn, meanwhile, was known as the "Toy Cannon." He was one of the Astros' only players who had enough power to consistently hit home runs in the large Astrodome. Wynn was only 160 pounds and stood 5-foot-10. But he hit 22 home runs in 1965. He then smashed 37 homers in 1967 to go along with 107 RBIs. He was named an NL All-Star that year.

Houston had improved. But Hofheinz wanted more improvement. Over the next few seasons, several of the team's top stars would be traded. These former Astros would blossom into superstars for their new teams. The deals kept Houston from fully reaching its potential in the 1970s.

CHAPTER 3

WHAT COULD HAVE BEEN

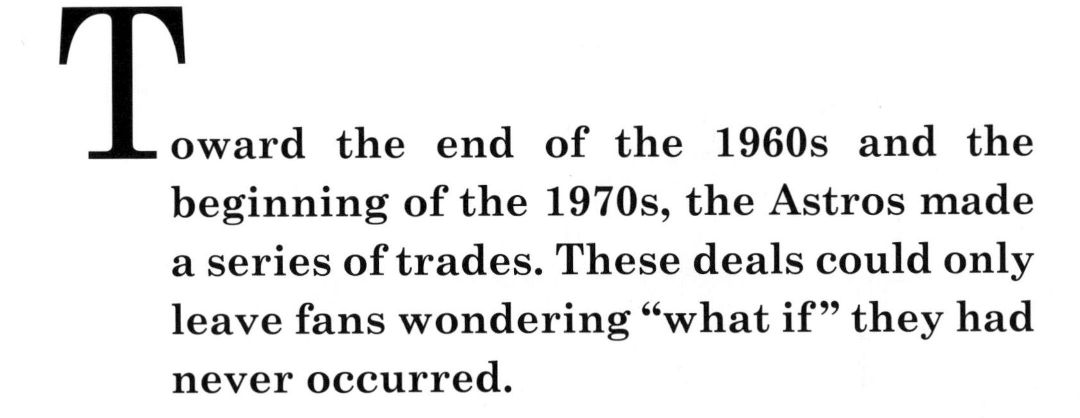

Toward the end of the 1960s and the beginning of the 1970s, the Astros made a series of trades. These deals could only leave fans wondering "what if" they had never occurred.

After the 1968 season, Rusty Staub was traded to the expansion Montreal Expos for three players. Staub had a breakout season with the Expos in 1969. He hit .302 with 29 home runs and 79 RBIs. He was a three-time All-Star with the club before being traded to the New York Mets in 1972.

Also after the 1968 season, the Astros shipped pitcher Mike Cuellar to the Baltimore Orioles for outfielder Curt Blefary and a minor league player. Blefary played only one season for Houston. Cuellar, meanwhile, became a star for Baltimore. He won the AL Cy Young Award in 1969 and helped the Orioles win

Houston second baseman Joe Morgan is shown in 1971. The Astros traded Morgan to the Reds after that season, and he helped Cincinnati win two World Series.

Next Willie Mays?

When Cesar Cedeno broke into the big leagues with the Astros, he had so many skills it left opposing managers amazed. Cedeno had the ability to hit for average and power, and his speed allowed him to steal bases easily. That speed also allowed him to cover a lot of ground in the outfield and make catches other center fielders could not. His strong right arm was also a weapon, as opposing base runners did not want to be thrown out trying to advance an extra base. His talent led some to compare him to the legendary Willie Mays. "I'm not saying he will be better than Mays. No way anybody can be better than Mays," said Leo Durocher, who managed the Astros in 1972 and 1973 and also managed Mays with the New York Giants in the 1950s. "But I will say this kid has a chance to be as good. And that's saying a lot."

the World Series in 1970. He won 20 games or more in a season four times with Baltimore.

The Astros then traded Joe Morgan, Jack Billingham, Ed Armbrister, Cesar Geronimo, and Denis Menke to the Cincinnati Reds after the 1971 season. Houston received Tommy Helms, Lee May, and Jimmy Stewart in exchange. Helms was steady in the field as a second baseman. But he was not a big contributor on offense. May, however, was a big offensive force. The first baseman averaged 27 home runs and 96 RBIs during his three seasons in Houston. Still, the trade was mostly known for helping turn Cincinnati into the "Big Red Machine."

The Reds lost in the World Series in 1972 before winning back-to-back titles in 1975 and 1976. Morgan was named the NL MVP for those two World Series-winning seasons. He was an eight-time All-Star with the Reds and was inducted into the Baseball Hall of Fame in 1990. Billingham, a tall right-handed pitcher, never had a

The Astros' Cesar Cedeno, *left*, gets up after stealing home in 1977. At right are Cubs catcher George Mitterwald and umpire Harry Wendelstedt.

losing season during his six years in Cincinnati. Geronimo, a center fielder, won four Gold Glove Awards with the Reds.

Despite the loss of so many stars, Houston had its best-ever season in 1972. The Astros went 84–69. Center fielder Cesar Cedeno had a big year. He batted .320, led the NL in doubles with 39, hit 22 home runs, and stole 55 bases. He also won a Gold Glove Award. Cedeno was named an NL All-Star from 1972 to 1974 and again in 1976. He won five straight Gold Gloves starting in 1972.

Those players—along with right-handed pitchers Larry Dierker and J. R. Richard,

Terry Puhl dances back to first base as the Giants' Jim Dwyer fields a pickoff attempt throw in 1978. Puhl was a key player for the new-look Astros in the late 1970s.

outfielder/first baseman Bob Watson, and third baseman Doug Rader—led the Astros. It seemed that Houston might overcome the poor trades from the previous seasons.

However, the 1975 season became one of transition. Pitcher Don Wilson tragically died at his home before the season. Houston struggled on the field. The Astros finished 64–97. The team averaged only 10,593 fans per game.

In financial trouble, the club changed owners. Tal Smith, who was with the club in its early days, was brought back to become the general manager.

Smith hired Bill Virdon as manager. Virdon had previously managed the Pittsburgh Pirates and the New York Yankees. Smith decided that Houston needed to focus on pitching, speed, and defense in order to play better in the spacious Astrodome. Smith also went on a trading frenzy. Outfielder Jose Cruz and pitcher Joe Niekro had been acquired before the 1975 season. After the 1975 season, Smith brought in pitcher Joaquin Andujar and third baseman/first baseman Art Howe.

During the 1977 season, outfielder Denny Walling was picked up from the Oakland Athletics. Catcher Alan Ashby, shortstop Craig Reynolds, infielder Rafael Landestoy, and outfielder Jeff Leonard were all acquired before the 1979 season. Rookie outfielder Terry Puhl joined the club in 1977. The team also brought up rookie catchers Bruce Bochy and Luis Pujols during the late 1970s. Smith's transformation of the club did not lead to immediate success on the field. But it laid the groundwork for the team's best run, starting in 1979.

Longtime Astro

Tal Smith has filled a variety of roles with Houston. He joined the club in 1960 as assistant to the new team's general manager. Heavily involved in the development and completion of the Astrodome, Smith became the vice president and director of player personnel in 1965. After leaving Houston for New York in 1973 to become the vice president of the Yankees, he returned to the Astros in 1975 as the team's general manager and became team president in 1976. After leaving the Astros after the 1980 season, Smith returned to the Astros in 1994 when he was named the team's president.

CHAPTER 4

FINALLY FINDING SUCCESS

After struggling to win during their first 17 years, the Astros began their first stretch of continued success in 1979. From 1979 through 1989, Houston recorded eight winning seasons and reached the playoffs three times.

The Astros went 89–73 in 1979. They were built around general manager Tal Smith's belief that pitching, speed, and defense win games. The team finished second in the NL West. Houston ranked last in the NL in runs scored and home runs. But the Astros were first in stolen bases.

Leading the pitching staff were starters J. R. Richard, Joe Niekro, Ken Forsch, and Joaquin Andujar as well as reliever Joe Sambito. Richard was one of the hardest throwers in baseball. He went 18–13 with a 2.71 ERA. He also led the NL with 313 strikeouts. Niekro finished 21–11 with a 3.00 ERA. As a

J. R. Richard gets ready to deliver a pitch in the late 1970s. In 1980, Richard went 10–4 before he was tragically sidelined by a stroke. The Astros still won their first division crown that year.

team, the Astros were second in the NL with a 3.20 ERA.

After the season, Houston signed free-agent pitcher Nolan Ryan. Ryan grew up in nearby Alvin, Texas. Ryan was said to have baseball's top fastball. He had become a star with the California Angels in the 1970s. He threw four no-hitters with California.

"Alvin Express"

During his 27-year big-league career, pitcher Nolan Ryan became a legend. One of his nicknames was the "Alvin Express"—named after his hometown of Alvin, Texas, and the speed of his pitches. Ryan finished his career with a major league-record 5,714 strikeouts. During his time with the California Angels, from 1972 to 1979, he threw four no-hitters and led the AL in strikeouts seven times. He topped 300 strikeouts in five of those seasons. After joining the Astros in 1980, he threw his record-breaking fifth no-hitter in 1981 and became baseball's all-time strikeout leader in 1983. After the 1988 season, he left the Astros and signed with the Texas Rangers. With the Rangers, he threw two more no-hitters. He retired after the 1993 season and finished his career with a 324–292 record. Ryan was inducted into the Baseball Hall of Fame in 1999 wearing a Rangers cap.

Astros fans believed that Houston was the team to beat in 1980. The Astros lived up to expectations. Cesar Cedeno had a team-best .309 batting average. Jose Cruz hit .302 and led Houston with 91 RBIs. The pitching, however, was the reason for the team's success. This was the case despite a tragic incident on July 30. On that day, Richard, who was 10–4 with a 1.90 ERA at the time, collapsed in the Astrodome during a workout. He suffered a stroke that cut off oxygen to the right side of his brain. Richard was near death. It took a series of operations to save his life.

Vern Ruhle replaced Richard in the rotation and finished

The Astros' Nolan Ryan prepares to fire a pitch in 1981. Ryan threw his record fifth career no-hitter in September of that year.

12–4 with a 2.37 ERA. The Astros' staff led the NL with a 3.10 ERA. Houston also ranked first in strikeouts.

Houston won 7–1 in a one-game playoff against the host Los Angeles Dodgers to capture the West Division title with a 93–70 record. The Astros then faced the Philadelphia Phillies in the NLCS. In a playoff series that included four extra-inning games, the Phillies won three games to two.

In 1981, the season was split into halves because of a players' strike. Ryan threw his record fifth no-hitter on September 26 in a 5–0 victory over the visiting Dodgers. This helped

Houston finish the second half of the season 33–20. The Astros won the NL West's second-half title. They advanced to face the Dodgers, the West's first-half champion, in a special division series. Houston again lost three games to two in a playoff series.

Houston failed to make the postseason from 1982 to 1985. In 1986, under the guidance of new manager Hal Lanier, the Astros returned to the postseason. Houston went 96–66 and easily won the NL West. Cruz, Denny Walling, and Terry Puhl were still important members of the team. But the offense was now led by first baseman Glenn Davis, right fielder Kevin Bass, second baseman Bill Doran, and center fielder Billy Hatcher.

Ryan, now 39 years old, went 12–8 with a 3.34 ERA. Bob Knepper finished 17–12 with a 3.14 ERA. The staff's ace, though, was Mike Scott. The right-hander went 18–10 and led the league in ERA (2.22) and strikeouts (306). He won the NL's Cy Young Award. On September 25, Scott threw a no-hitter against the visiting San Francisco Giants to clinch the NL West title.

The Astros faced the New York Mets in the NLCS. Scott

A Fallen Giant

J. R. Richard towered over opposing hitters, standing 6-foot-8. He was the first right-hander to strike out more than 300 hitters in the NL, accomplishing the feat in 1978 and again in 1979. Sadly, Richard's career was cut short when he experienced a stroke on July 30, 1980. The stroke required a life-saving operation, and then he needed a second operation that lasted 18 hours. Though he vowed to make a comeback and did pitch during training camp in 1981, Richard was never able to return to the big leagues. He finished his career with a record of 107–71 in parts of 10 big-league seasons, all with Houston.

Mike Scott celebrates after pitching a three-hitter to lift the Astros to a 3–1 win over the Mets in Game 4 of the 1986 NLCS. Houston lost the series in six games.

shut out New York 1–0 in Game 1 while striking out 14. He also was a complete-game winner in Houston's 3–1 victory in Game 4. The Mets prevailed in the series when they won 7–6 in 16 innings in an epic Game 6 in the Astrodome. Even though the Astros lost the series, Scott was named its MVP.

Houston had put together a special season in 1986. But the Astros would not return to the playoffs for several years.

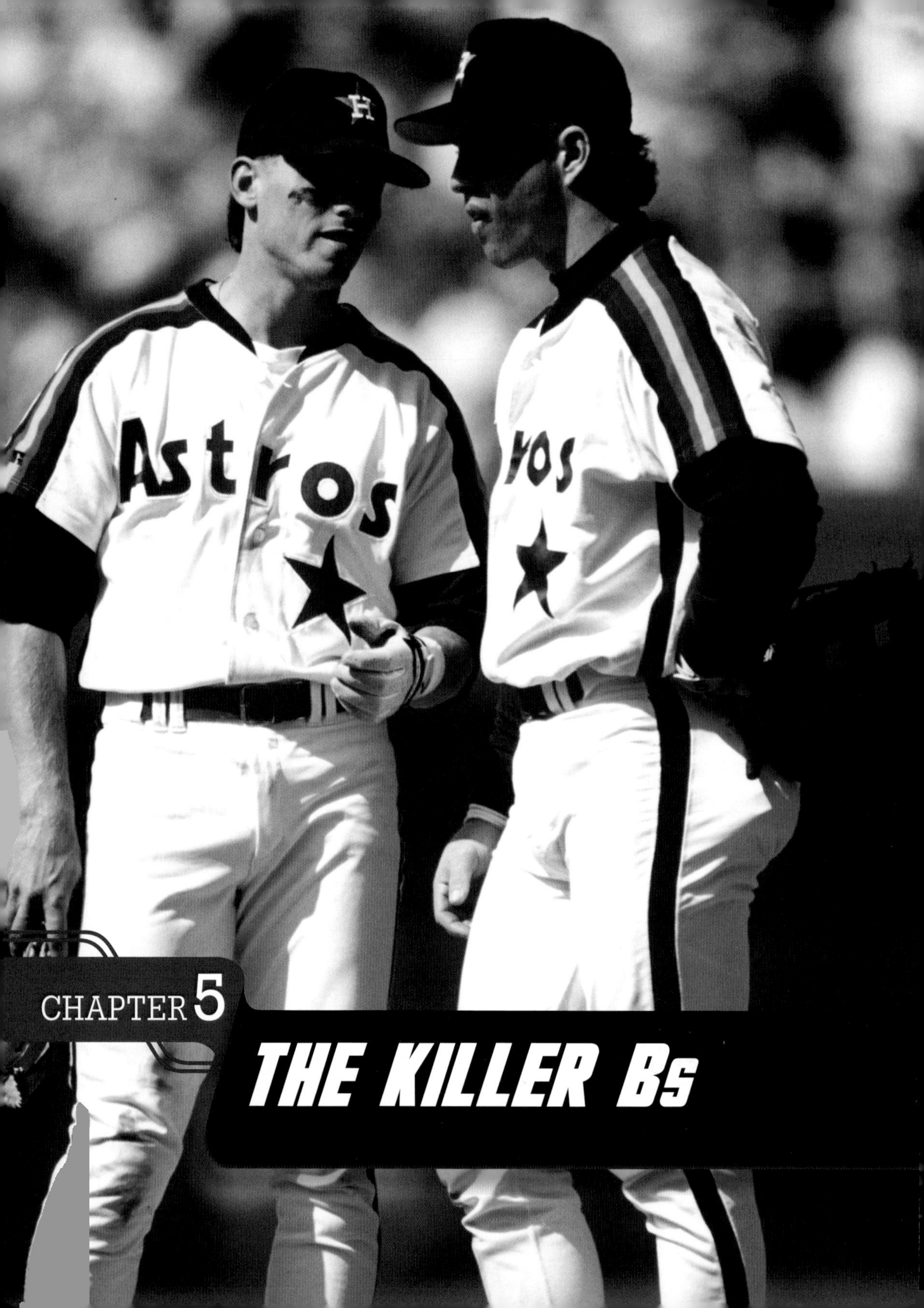

CHAPTER 5

THE KILLER Bs

The thrill of 1986 quickly disappeared for the Astros. The team suffered losing seasons in 1987, 1990, and 1991. But during the down period, two players would emerge to turn Houston's fate around.

Craig Biggio appeared in 50 games in 1988. He then became Houston's starting catcher in 1989. Two years later, Jeff Bagwell made his debut as a first baseman for the Astros. Together, Biggio and Bagwell would lead the way for the Astros for the next 15 years. Both players spent their entire careers with Houston. They appear at or toward the top of several team offensive-record lists.

Biggio finished his career with 3,060 hits. He appeared in seven All-Star Games and won four Gold Glove Awards. After

Second baseman Craig Biggio, *left*, and first baseman Jeff Bagwell talk in 1992. The two stars played together for Houston from 1991 to 2005.

breaking in as a catcher, he moved to second base in 1992 before shifting to center field and left field in 2003 and 2004. He then went back to playing second base from 2005 to 2007. Biggio became the first big-league player ever to be named an All-Star at catcher one year, in 1991, and at second base the next year.

The Astros acquired Bagwell from the Boston Red Sox on August 30, 1990. They sent relief pitcher Larry Andersen to Boston. The trade would prove to be a steal for Houston. Bagwell was a third baseman in the minor leagues. But with Ken Caminiti at third, the Astros moved Bagwell to first base during spring training in 1991. That season, Bagwell hit .294 with 15 home runs and 82 RBIs to win the NL Rookie of the Year Award. Each year, he gained more power. In the strike-shortened 1994 season, he hit .368 with 39 homers and 116 RBIs in 110 games. He was named NL MVP. That year, Houston joined the Central Division in a realigned NL.

Linked Together

Craig Biggio and Jeff Bagwell are often mentioned together. The duo played with each other from 1991 to 2005. Through 2010, Biggio was the Astros' all-time leader in games played (2,850), at-bats (10,876), runs scored (1,844), and hits (3,060). He also set a major league record by getting hit by a pitch 285 times. Bagwell was Houston's all-time leader in home runs (449), RBIs (1,529), and walks (1,401).

The Astros had become winners again. Biggio and Bagwell led the way on offense. Darryl Kile, Mike Hampton, and Shane Reynolds guided the pitching staff. After going 81–81 in 1992, Houston recorded seven straight winning seasons. From 1994 to 1996, the

Larry Dierker, shown in 1999, managed the Astros to four division titles from 1997 to 2001. But the team did not win a playoff series under him.

Astros finished second in the NL Central. They added outfielder Derek Bell in 1995 and third baseman Sean Berry in 1996. Those two players along with Bagwell and Biggio became known as "the Killer Bs." In 1997, Larry Dierker was named manager. The former Houston pitcher had been serving as a television analyst for the club. Even though Dierker was a first-time manager, the Astros won the NL Central at 84–78. The Astros, though, were swept in three games in the playoffs' first round, the NLDS, by the Atlanta Braves.

In 1998, the Astros put together their best regular

Randy Johnson prepares to release a pitch in 1998. Johnson was dominant during his short stay with the Astros after the team acquired him during the season that year.

season in team history. Before the season, Houston acquired outfielder Moises Alou from the Florida Marlins. With Alou joining the Killer Bs, the offense flourished. Bagwell, Bell, and Alou each drove in more than 100 runs. Biggio joined those three to give the Astros four players with 20 or more home runs that season. Biggio also had 50 steals and 51 doubles.

Reynolds paced the pitching staff. He went 19–8 with a 3.51 ERA. Before the trade deadline in July, the Astros acquired ace left-hander Randy Johnson from the Seattle Mariners. Johnson dominated the NL after joining the Astros. He went 10–1 with a 1.28 ERA. This helped Houston set a club mark for wins at 102–60.

But as was the case in four previous trips to the postseason, the Astros failed to win a series. Thanks in part to outstanding pitching from Kevin Brown, the Padres upset the Astros in the NLDS. San Diego won three games to one. Johnson left to join the Arizona Diamondbacks after the season. But Houston returned most of its key players in 1999. The Astros once again won the Central Division, at 97–65. Houston defeated the Los Angeles Dodgers 9–4 on the final day of the regular season to clinch the division title. It was the last regular-season game ever played in the Astrodome. Unfortunately for the Astros, the trend of losing in the playoffs continued. Houston fell three games to one to Atlanta in the NLDS.

The end of the decade not only meant the end of the Astrodome as the home of the Astros. It also was the end of the most successful run in team history. After going 65–97 in 1991, Houston did not suffer a losing season during the rest of the 1990s and won three division titles. This was due in no small part to the All-Star play and leadership provided by Bagwell and Biggio.

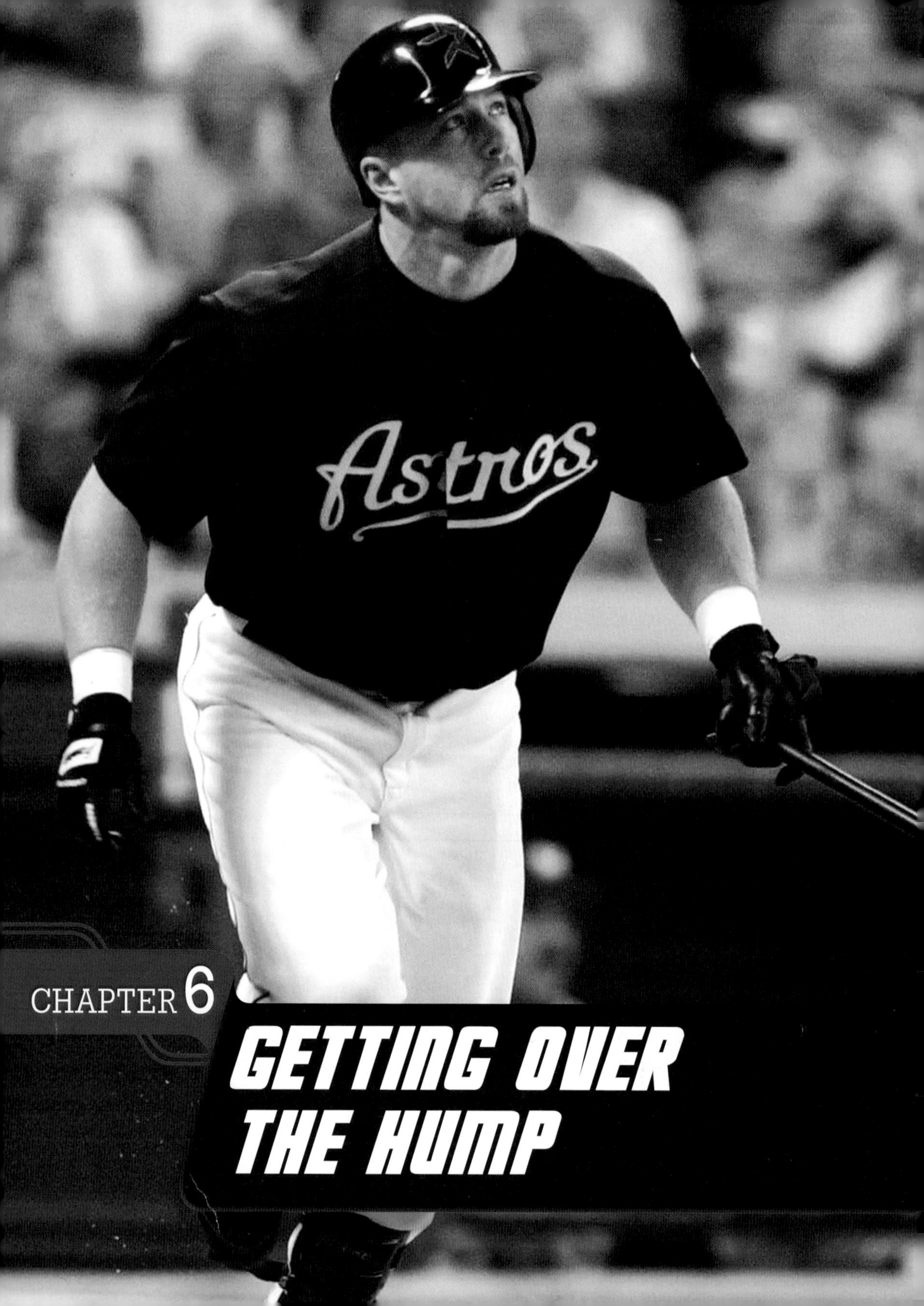

CHAPTER 6

GETTING OVER THE HUMP

The Astrodome was known as the "Eighth Wonder of the World." It had protected Houston's baseball players and fans from the humid summer weather. In 2000, the team moved into a new stadium—Enron Field—that had a retractable roof. This meant that the fans could enjoy outdoor baseball during favorable weather.

Center field at the new stadium was a distant 436 feet from home plate. But the ball flew out of the park down the lines and in the power alleys. As a result, the Astros hit an NL-record 249 home runs in 2000. Jeff Bagwell had a team-record 47 homers. Richard Hidalgo emerged with 44. Moises Alou belted 30. Rookie Lance Berkman added 21.

The pitchers struggled in the new park, however. The staff gave up 234 homers in 2000. With the pitchers unable to adjust to Enron Field, the Astros fell to 72–90.

Jeff Bagwell watches one of the career-high 47 homers he belted in 2000. That year, the Astros moved into a new stadium, Enron Field, that was friendly to hitters.

But Houston's pitching staff bounced back in 2001. Shane Reynolds, second-year starter Wade Miller, and rookie Roy Oswalt showed the way. The Astros finished 93–69 and won the Central Division.

As in 1997 and 1999, the Astros faced the Atlanta Braves in the NLDS. The Braves knocked the Astros out of the postseason yet again, winning the series in three games.

For whatever reason, Houston was unable to get past the first round of the playoffs. The NLDS loss to Atlanta in 2001 cost manager Larry Dierker his job. Jimy Williams was hired as the next manager. In 2002, Houston's home stadium was renamed Minute Maid Park. The Astros failed to make the playoffs in 2002 and 2003. The club had high expectations heading into 2004, though. Before that season, the Astros signed Houston-area natives Roger Clemens and Andy Pettitte. Pettitte was only able to start 15 games before he was sidelined with an arm injury. But the staff still had Oswalt and Clemens. The offense had All-Stars in Bagwell, Berkman, Carlos Beltran, Craig Biggio, and Jeff Kent. Yet, after 88 games, the Astros were 44–44.

Owner Drayton McLane replaced Williams with former

2004 All-Star Game

Minute Maid Park was the site of the 2004 Major League All-Star Game. Even though the Astros were only 44–44 at the All-Star break, four of their players made the NL All-Star team. Jeff Kent and Lance Berkman started at second base and in center field, respectively. Roger Clemens was the starting pitcher. Outfielder Carlos Beltran, who began the season with the Kansas City Royals before being acquired by the Astros on June 24, was a reserve for the NL team.

Center fielder Carlos Beltran tips his cap as his teammates celebrate in the background. Houston had just beaten Atlanta in the 2004 NLDS for its first playoff series win in team history.

Astros player Phil Garner as manager. Houston went 48–26 the rest of the year. The team finished 92–70 and earned the NL's wild-card playoff spot. Clemens went 18–4 with a 2.98 ERA. He won the NL Cy Young Award. Oswalt finished 20–10 and was third in the Cy Young voting.

Once again, Houston would face Atlanta in the NLDS. The series went to a Game 5 showdown. Beltran hit two homers. Bagwell also homered. Houston won 12–3 and earned the first playoff series victory in team history.

The Astros advanced to face the division rival St. Louis

Cardinals in the NLCS. The Astros took a three-games-to-two lead with a 3–0 victory in Game 5. Kent hit a game-winning, three-run homer in the ninth inning.

However, with the series back in St. Louis, the Cardinals prevailed 6–4 in 12 innings in Game 6 and 5–2 in Game 7.

The following season, 2005, the Astros made a major comeback after a slow start. They again won the NL's wild-card berth and beat the Braves in the NLDS. They also took the next step, however. They defeated the Cardinals in the NLCS to advance to the team's first World Series. There, Houston ran into an even hotter team. The Chicago White Sox ended the Astros' dream season with a Series sweep.

As of 2010, the Astros had not been back to the postseason since their 2005 World Series defeat. They were a team in transition, seeking to find another winning formula.

Bagwell spent the entire 2006 season on the disabled list and retired at the end of the season. Biggio collected his 3,000th career hit during the

Beltran's Big Postseason

During the 2004 postseason, Carlos Beltran showed baseball fans everywhere just how well he was capable of playing. In the NLDS against Atlanta, Beltran hit .455 with four home runs, nine RBIs, nine runs, and two stolen bases in five games. Beltran continued his outstanding hitting during the NLCS against St. Louis. In seven games, he batted .417 with four homers, five RBIs, 12 runs, and four stolen bases. At 6-foot-1 and 190 pounds, Beltran did not look like a power hitter, but his power was deceptive. Beltran became a free agent at the end of the 2004 season. The New York Mets made the switch-hitting center fielder an offer he could not refuse, and he decided to leave the Astros for the Mets. As of 2010, he was still with New York.

The Astros' Hunter Pence follows through after connecting for a home run in 2010. Pence finished the season with 25 homers and 91 RBIs.

2007 season and then retired. Just like that, the Astros' two icons were gone.

In 2010, two more Astros stars said good-bye to the team. The team traded Oswalt to the Philadelphia Phillies and Berkman to the New York Yankees.

By the end of 2010, a different group of players was leading Houston. Right fielder Hunter Pence hit 25 homers for the third straight season. Center fielder Michael Bourn continued to be one of the NL's top base stealers. With the help of those two, the Astros would continue to shoot for the stars and seek the team's first World Series title.

TIMELINE

1962	The expansion Houston Colt .45s play their first game, facing the Chicago Cubs at Colt Stadium on April 10. Houston defeats the Cubs 11–2 and goes on to sweep the three-game series to start 3–0 as a team.
1965	Now called the Astros after changing the team name, Houston loses its first game in its new stadium, the Astrodome, on April 12. Houston falls 2–0 to the Philadelphia Phillies.
1973	The Astros' Cesar Cedeno becomes the first player in major league history to record at least 50 steals and 20 home runs in back-to-back seasons.
1980	The Astros capture their first division championship, beating the Los Angeles Dodgers 7–1 in a one-game playoff on October 6 to win the West Division title. Houston then loses three games to two to Philadelphia in the NLCS.
1981	Nolan Ryan throws the fifth no-hitter of his career in the Astros' 5–0 home victory over the Dodgers on September 26. In a season split into halves because of a players' strike, Houston wins the NL West's second-half title. The Astros then fall three games to two to the Dodgers in a special division playoff series.
1986	On September 25, Mike Scott, that year's NL Cy Young Award winner, throws a no-hitter against the visiting San Francisco Giants. This lifts the Astros to a 2–0 victory and clinches the West Division title for them. In the NLCS, the Astros fall four games to two to the New York Mets. In Game 6, Houston loses a 3–0 lead in the ninth inning and ends up falling 7–6 in 16 innings.

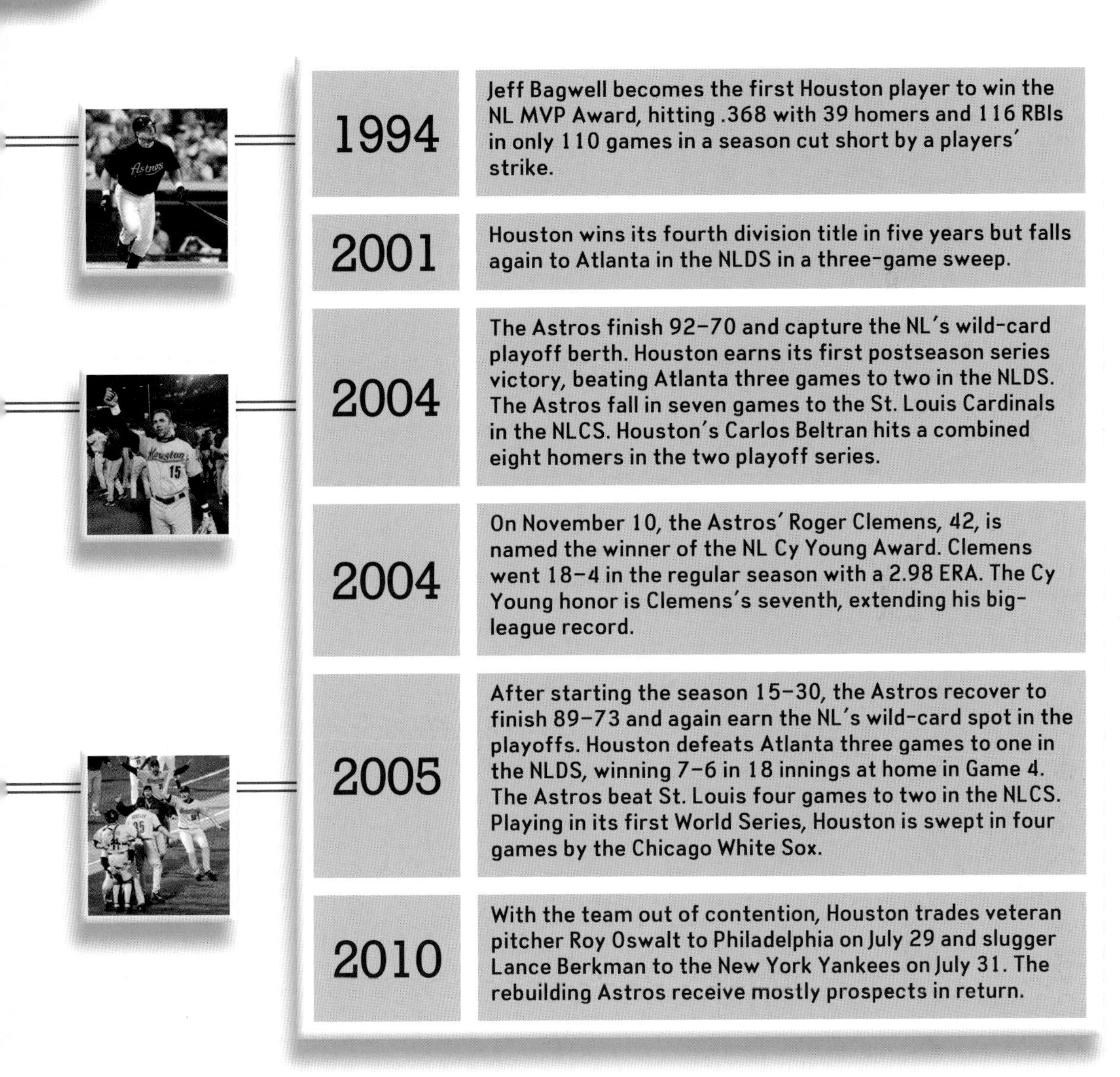

1994	Jeff Bagwell becomes the first Houston player to win the NL MVP Award, hitting .368 with 39 homers and 116 RBIs in only 110 games in a season cut short by a players' strike.
2001	Houston wins its fourth division title in five years but falls again to Atlanta in the NLDS in a three-game sweep.
2004	The Astros finish 92–70 and capture the NL's wild-card playoff berth. Houston earns its first postseason series victory, beating Atlanta three games to two in the NLDS. The Astros fall in seven games to the St. Louis Cardinals in the NLCS. Houston's Carlos Beltran hits a combined eight homers in the two playoff series.
2004	On November 10, the Astros' Roger Clemens, 42, is named the winner of the NL Cy Young Award. Clemens went 18–4 in the regular season with a 2.98 ERA. The Cy Young honor is Clemens's seventh, extending his big-league record.
2005	After starting the season 15–30, the Astros recover to finish 89–73 and again earn the NL's wild-card spot in the playoffs. Houston defeats Atlanta three games to one in the NLDS, winning 7–6 in 18 innings at home in Game 4. The Astros beat St. Louis four games to two in the NLCS. Playing in its first World Series, Houston is swept in four games by the Chicago White Sox.
2010	With the team out of contention, Houston trades veteran pitcher Roy Oswalt to Philadelphia on July 29 and slugger Lance Berkman to the New York Yankees on July 31. The rebuilding Astros receive mostly prospects in return.

QUICK STATS

FRANCHISE HISTORY

Houston Colt .45s (1962–64)
Houston Astros (1965–)

WORLD SERIES

2005

NL CHAMPIONSHIP SERIES *(1969–)*

1980, 1986, 2004, 2005

DIVISION CHAMPIONSHIPS *(1969–)*

1980, 1981 (second-half title), 1986, 1997, 1998, 1999, 2001

KEY PLAYERS *(position[s]; seasons with team)*

Jeff Bagwell (1B; 1991–2005)
Lance Berkman (OF/1B; 1999–2010)
Craig Biggio (C/2B/OF; 1988–2007)
Cesar Cedeno (OF; 1970–81)
Roger Clemens (SP; 2004–06)
Jose Cruz (OF; 1975–87)
Larry Dierker (SP; 1964–76)
Joe Morgan (2B; 1963–71, 1980)
Joe Niekro (SP; 1975–85)
Roy Oswalt (SP; 2001–10)
J. R. Richard (SP; 1971–80)
Nolan Ryan (SP; 1980–88)
Mike Scott (SP; 1983–91)
Don Wilson (SP; 1966–74)
Jimmy Wynn (OF; 1963–73)

KEY MANAGERS

Larry Dierker (1997–2001):
435–348; 2–12 (postseason)
Phil Garner (2004–07):
277–252; 13–13 (postseason)
Bill Virdon (1975–82):
544–522; 4–6 (postseason)

HOME PARKS

Colt Stadium (1962–64)
Astrodome (1965–99)
Minute Maid Park (2000–)
Known as Enron Field (2000–01)

* All statistics through 2010 season

QUOTES AND ANECDOTES

"I tried to stay focused, but you get a standing ovation every single time up there, it's a nice appreciation. I'm very grateful, really thankful, for a lot of things. A lot of things have happened here over the course of my 20-year career, but tonight I think was the best. I'm just glad we finally got it done."
—Longtime Astro Craig Biggio, after collecting his 3,000th career hit on June 28, 2007. Biggio went 5-for-6 in Houston's 8–5 victory in 11 innings over the visiting Colorado Rockies. His single, in which he was thrown out trying to stretch it into a double, in the seventh inning was hit number 3,000. He added singles in the ninth and 11th innings.

"The nice thing about Cedeno is that he can play all three outfield positions—at the same time."
—Montreal Expos manager Gene Mauch, talking about speedy Astros center fielder Cesar Cedeno

"It takes him an hour and a half to watch *60 Minutes*."
—Donald Davidson, Astros executive, on Houston pitcher Joe Niekro's relaxed nature

In 2009, the Astros became the first team in major league history to have three players who hit their 300th home run in the same season. Ivan Rodriguez was the first Astro to reach that milestone on May 17 at Wrigley Field in Chicago. Lance Berkman followed on June 13 at Arizona, and Carlos Lee reached number 300 on August 8 at Minute Maid Park. Rodriguez also set a major league record by catching his 2,227th career game on June 17 at Texas.

GLOSSARY

ace

A team's best starting pitcher.

acquire

To receive a player through trade or by signing as a free agent.

berth

A place, spot, or position, such as in the baseball playoffs.

clinch

To officially settle something, such as a berth in the playoffs.

expansion

In sports, to add a franchise or franchises to a league.

franchise

An entire sports organization, including the players, coaches, and staff.

free agent

A player free to sign with any team of his choosing after his contract expires.

general manager

The executive who is in charge of the team's overall operation. He or she hires and fires managers and coaches, drafts players, and signs free agents.

postseason

Games played in the playoffs by the top teams after the regular-season schedule has been completed.

retire

To officially end one's career.

retractable

Can be opened or closed mechanically depending on the weather.

rookie

A first-year professional athlete.

veteran

An individual with great experience in a particular endeavor.

wild card

Playoff berths given to the best remaining teams that did not win their respective divisions.

FOR MORE INFORMATION

Further Reading

Dierker, Larry. *This Ain't Brain Surgery: How to Win the Pennant Without Losing Your Mind*. New York: Simon & Schuster, 2003.

Ortiz, Jose de Jesus. *Houston Astros: Armed and Dangerous*. Champaign, IL: Sports Publishing LLC, 2006.

Vecsey, George. *Baseball: A History of America's Favorite Game*. New York: Modern Library, 2008.

Web Links

To learn more about the Houston Astros, visit ABDO Publishing Company online at **www.abdopublishing.com**. Web sites about the Astros are featured on our Book Links page. These links are routinely monitored and updated to provide the most current information available.

Places to Visit

Astros Spring Training
Osceola County Stadium
631 Heritage Park Way
Kissimmee, FL 34744
321-697-3201
www.osceolastadium.com
Located near the Disney World theme parks, Osceola County Stadium has been the spring-training home of the Astros since 1985.

Minute Maid Park
501 Crawford Street
Houston, TX 77002
713-259-8000
http://mlb.mlb.com/hou/ballpark/index.jsp
Minute Maid Park has been home to the Astros since 2000. The team plays 81 regular-season games here each year.

National Baseball Hall of Fame and Museum
25 Main Street
Cooperstown, NY 13326
1-888-HALL-OF-FAME
www.baseballhall.org
This hall of fame and museum highlights the greatest players and moments in the history of baseball. Joe Morgan and Nolan Ryan are among the former Astros enshrined here.

INDEX

About the Author

J Chris Roselius is an award-winning journalist and writer. A graduate of the University of Texas, he has written numerous books. Roselius resides in Houston with his wife and two children.